CW01652385

Beulah

A play

James Robson

Samuel French — London
New York - Toronto - Hollywood

ISBN 0 573 01726 3

Please see page iv for further copyright information

BEULAH

First performed at the Old Meeting House, Hemsley, North Yorkshire, by the 1812 Theatre Company on 17th November 1994, with the following cast:

Dad (Jack Ling)	Howard Burnham
Mam (Lottie Ling)	Margaret Wootton
Rene	Mary Tate
Heather	Lucinda Barnes
Evie	Margot Simpson
Mary	Julie Thompson
Craig	Andy Head/Steve Hick
Frank	Glyn Price
Gary	Charles Saggers
Alice	Moira Wood

Directed by John Allen
Staged-managed by Mark Brydon and Rosalind de Aragues
Set constructed by Geoff Preston and Alan Magson
Lighting by Stuart Hague and Terry Johnson

(See also page ii)

CHARACTERS

Dad (Jack Ling)
Mam (Lottie Ling), Jack's wife
Rene, Jack's and Lottie's daughter
Heather, her sister
Evie, her sister
Mary, her sister
Craig, Jack's and Lottie's son
Frank, Jack's brother
Garry, Mary's son
Alice, Resident Warden

The action takes place in the living-room of Dad's and Mam's bungalow in an old folks' sheltered estate in a North Yorkshire market town

SYNOPSIS OF SCENES

ACT I, Scene 1 A Sunday evening in Spring
Scene 2 Afternoon, a month later
Scene 3 Afternoon, a week later

ACT II, Scene 1 Afternoon, three days later
Scene 2 Later that night
Scene 3 Three months later, morning
Scene 4 Two months later, morning

Time — 1993

AUTHOR'S NOTE

Set

The set can be minimalist/representational — for example, it could be contained by wooden frames which open like a book, or simply staged against any interior wall with exits. Whatever, the general effect should be unsettling rather than cosy. We should have a sense of lives reduced, diminished: the Lings' hearts are elsewhere, they are people who once lived in a broader, brighter place.

Music

Between the scenes, pastoral music might be played, for example, Ralph Vaughan Williams's *Six Studies in English Folk Music*.

James Robson

NOTES ON THE CHARACTERS

Dad

Jack Ling. Aged 70. An ex-farmer and Dalesman, once a powerhouse of work and stamina, now wasted by age and cancer. A limited but kind, generous, honest and patient man, strict and of simple faith. A loving father and devoted husband — proud of his prolific strain. A serious, careful *countryman* who is losing his powerful grip on life at last. His moods range from dreamy childish dependence to anger, self-assertion, sad nostalgia, and finally, religious exultation.

Frank

Jack's brother. Aged 67. Physically similar to Jack if possible but very different in character and constitution; where Jack is sober and thoughtful, Frank is lively, full of rather old-fashioned fun, louder, and a bit of a rural wag and ladies' man, though never lecherous. He is an old charmer, a bachelor who bears an undertow of disappointment beneath his surface froth. A relentless tease in his day, in the peculiarly Yorkshire way.

Mam

Lottie Ling. Jack's wife. Aged 66. An indomitable Yorkshire woman. A restless, dissatisfied person whose once vivacious nature has been blunted over the years by hard work, age, and lack of personal fulfilment. If she was born today she would probably become an artist or career-person. Instead she tied herself to a man who worshipped and won her but never quite fired her nature — a man she respected and was very fond of but who never became her soul-mate. Her mind remains acute and she is still pugnacious — ready to meet life head-on. Hard-bitten, with a grudge against the world, but soft-centred and shrewd in the mould of Hannah Hauxwell. Mam can be charming when she chooses and extremely, outrageously funny — but she would rather argue than agree.

Rene

First-born daughter. Aged 49. She is married and has two children and a grandchild. Rene has always been the good girl — her mother's little helper and her father's particular favourite; the first, obedient, loyal, loving Daddy's girl of the family. A constant giver, an optimist just beginning to be puzzled by a tincture of sadness, of doubt.

Heather
Aged 47. She is married and has children of her own but doesn't completely love her husband. The great love her basically romantic soul longed for has not come along, which has made her cynical and impatient of all such high-flown notions in others. Heather likes to think, and portray herself as tough, rather witty, and full of bitter experience. She is still attractive and vivacious although there is a trace of desperation in her at times. Oddly, she is the one her parents take most for granted and expect to do most for their everyday needs. Though all the sisters were brought up to sing in chapel, Heather has the only natural and true singing voice.

Evie
Aged 45. Once the black sheep of the family for joining the WRAC and coming home discharged and pregnant, she now lives "down South" with the transgressor husband. Evie is superficially unlike her sisters, larger both physically and mentally: a good-time Northern girl transformed by her own desire and artifice into a respectable Harrow housewife. She seems tough but is really soft-hearted, generous, fun, likeable and funny. She is touched only now and then by the loneliness of her Southern exile and the fact that her husband is a compulsive womanizer. Her marriage has become an arrangement for financial reasons and "for the kids' sake". Evie knows that her life has been misdirected but has made a brave fist of it anyway. She is glossier than her sisters and more broad-minded. She dresses better than them and speaks with an acquired suburban Middlesex drone.

Mary
Aged 43. A born brave loser. Mary resembles Mam most of all and hates the fact. She is scruffy, thin, worn — a bit of a female hippie whose early wildness and sense of the artistic have degenerated into a kind of dated, odd response to situations. Living on the State in a run-down council house, she remains courageous, still trying to salvage something from the mess she has been reduced to. Attracted to hopeless, feckless men — she has four children from two fathers — she finds herself drawn to naïve causes; having managed to extricate herself from the Jehovah's Witnesses she is tentatively seeking salvation in the Women's Movement. She is the desperate head of her fierce one-parent (as she ruefully calls it) "brood".

Garry
Member of Mary's brood. Aged 16. Streetwise, SEGA and comic mad. Always chewing gum. Practically non-speaking role.

Craig
Aged 40. The only son and the one who did well at school, earned a scholarship and left home. A rather uneasy, dry, fairly diffident, detached man most of the time, he is really self-centred, quite ruthless yet emotional and prone to nostalgic binges whenever he returns to the family hearth. He is just getting over the failure of his second marriage and the inevitable period of self-examination and justification. Rumpled, occasionally droll, and rather world-weary now. He is a staff photographer with one of the national newspapers. Doted upon by Mam.

Alice
Aged 60-65. Warden of the sheltered estate where the Lings live. A brisk, no-nonsense woman, lacking in many fine feelings.

ACT I

Scene 1

The cramped living-room of an old folks' bungalow in a North Yorkshire market town; one of a dozen or so similar dwellings controlled by the Resident Warden. Sunday evening, March 1993

There is a large window with lace curtains looking out on to a garden or lawns. There are two doors, one leading to the kitchen and bedroom, the other leading to the main entrance. There are three imaginatively painted plaster ducks in wonky flight on the wall, a grandfather clock, an old couch or chaise-longue, *four farmhouse chairs of some antiquity (one of carver type), and an old wind-up gramophone circa 1950, with a few 78 records. At the back of the room, and dominating it somewhat, hangs a very big, professionally blown-up photograph (sepia, tinted or black and white but not colour) of "Beulah", a stone and pan-tiled farmhouse nestling on the wooded slope of a North Yorkshire Dale*

The curtains are drawn. The room is resounding with the voices of Rene, Heather and Mary who are singing, gathered around Dad's blanketed figure lying on the couch. Dad is in his pyjamas and propped on cushions; he sings too, while staring up at the photo of "Beulah" on the wall. He conducts with a frail white arm. Mam is seated in a chair knitting, looking deeply and defiantly bored. In a chair opposite sits Garry, reading a Judge Dredd *comic. He is listening to a Walkman and chewing gum*

Rene
Heather
Mary
Dad } *(together; singing)*

When the roll is called up yonder
When the roll is called up yonder
When the roll is called up yonder
When the roll is called up yonder I'll be there!

Mam glares at them and shakes her head

On that bright and cloudless morning
When the dead in Christ shall rise
And the glory of his resurrection share
When his chosen ones shall gather to their home beyond the skies

And the roll is called up yonder I'll be there!
I'll be there, I'll be there
When the roll is called up yonder I'll be there.

The song ends and Dad beams at his daughters

Mam I won't be there.

The women laugh

Dad Course you will, Lottie love, we'll all be there.
Mam I don't want to be there.
Dad You're just saying that.
Mam If all them sanctimonious lot are going to be there I think'll be there — your side of the family for instance — I'd rather go to hell.
Dad Now, Lottie, it's Sunday.
Mam I hate Sundays, always have. (*She stops knitting and cocks an ear to the wall*) 'Er next door'll be knocking again, she's got her telly on full blast.
Rene (*putting a hand on Dad's arm*) Maybe we ought to stop now, Dad?

Dad sighs then smiles

Dad I have enjoyed it, lasses.
Mam (*snorting*) It's worn you out, laid on your back behaving like Sir Malcolm Sargent——
Heather We always used to have a singsong on Sunday nights, Mam ...
Dad At Beulah — (*he stares up at the picture*) ay.
Mam We're not up at Beulah now, there's not just badgers and foxes sat listening outside.

Mam resumes knitting. Heather sits up like an attentive rabbit behind Mam's back

Heather An' wabbits, Mam? Were wabbits wistening?
Mam I'm a heathen, I don't like hymns — I'd rather listen to pop music like Darren there ...

The women giggle. Mam looks at Garry. Garry chews

Mary (*correcting her wearily*) Garry, Mam — that's Garry.
Dad Just one more, lasses, then we'll pack in.

Heather "Jesus wants me for a Sunbeam"?

They laugh. Mam glares at the wall

Mam You can laugh, she'll be knocking again — she'll be complaining to the warder.
Rene Ward*en*, Mam ...
Mam I know what I mean, our Rene, don't correct me.
Dad We'll leave it now, lasses, been grand.

Heather drifts to the window, Mary to the chair between Mam and Garry where she stares at Mam's knitting. Rene stays beside Dad, stroking his forehead

Mam (*noticing Mary's stare*) It's for your Wayne.

Mary just stares

Balaclava.

Garry stops chewing. Mary mouths: "It's for Wayne". Garry chews on

Dad What was that?
Mam Balaclava! I'm making Wayne a balaclava!
Dad Wayne who?
Mam Our Mary's Wayne with the big ears!

Mary sighs. Heather smirks

Mary How is he, Mam?
Mam (*glancing at Dad*) He goes in spasms, one day you can't get a chirp out of him, next you can't shut him up.
Dad Our Craig should have had a lad to carry the family name on.
Mam There's time yet.
Mary (*drily*) Third time lucky maybe.
Rene Poor Craig, he hasn't much luck with women ——
Mam Women aren't women these days. (*She snorts*) These femininin*in*ists. They want shaking up in a sack.

The women grin at each other in irritated fondness. Dad stares up at Beulah. Mam holds up the semblance of a balaclava in shocking red wool

What d'you think?

The women stare, gobstruck

Heather They'll see him coming anyway.

They laugh. Mam snorts and knits on

Mam He'll be glad of it cold winter mornings.

Pause. Garry inspects his gum, replaces it and chews on

Dad Nineteen forty-seven. That was a bad winter, Lottie.

Mam ignores this and continues with her knitting

I had to dig a tunnel out to cowshed to do milking.

Rene Yes, Dad.

Dad Me and our Frank pulled the milk sled on to village for groceries. (*Pause*) You could touch pots on top of telegraph poles if you made a long arm.

Mary Has Craig written lately?

Mam shakes her head as if she didn't want to hear this

Dad Worst winter in living memory. Sheep on Scartops got their eyes picked out by crows. Laid wi' their heads out of drifts like great red chrysanths when me and Frank reached 'em. We'd bagged some hay, carried it through snow up to our bellies. Frank said he could see nowt but blue shapes when he blinked — sun was hot but air was like a knife at back of your throat. (*He suddenly becomes agitated, and feels amongst the blankets for something*)

Rene What is it, Dad?

Dad I can't find my pipe, Rene lass ...

Rene looks for it as well. Heather moves closer to Mam

Heather (*to Mam*) Have you hidden it again?

Mam Doctor said he hasn't to have it. Pipe, pipe, where's my pipe all day — I don't know where the mucky old thing is!

Heather searches the couch with Rene

Mam Badly weaned that's his trouble. Got to have something stuck in his mouth.
Mary (*absently*) They're all the same.
Mam His mother must've had a bad teat!

Heather and Mary laugh ruefully. Dad laughs along with them obligingly

Rene That's not a nice thing to say, Mam ——
Mam (*mischievously now*) Old Violet Ling. Come to think, she had two bad uns — seen bigger bee stings!
Rene *Mam* ——
Mam (*reproved*) Well. She hated my bosoms — she used to stare at them as if she wished they'd drop off.

Pause

I had some bosoms.

After a brisk knock on the outer door, the Resident Warden, Alice, enters, smiling falsely, with Frank in tow

Alice Evening, Lottie, evening, girls! Frank's here. (*She beams across at Dad*) How's my fancy man this evening? (*Before he can reply*) Good. How are you, Lottie, love?
Mam Waiting to die same as rest.
Alice (*laughing falsely*) Isn't she a character? She's so independent, aren't you love?
Mam I'm not brain-damaged you know — I'm same as I was thirty year ago only older.
Alice (*to the others*) She won't come to any of our "dos" at the Elderberry Club. There's a Domino Drive tomorrow night, Lottie ——
Mam Have a nice time.
Mary Why don't you join in a bit more, Mam?
Mam I hate old people. (*She glances at Frank*) You can sit down, it's same price as standing.
Frank (*doing so*) Ay, can't stay long — just called in on my way out like.
Mam On your way t' pub?
Frank Ay. (*Grinning*) Now then, lasses — you're in good voice tonight.
Rene Now then, Uncle Frank, how're you?
Frank Grand, Rene lass ...
Mam Never out of pub so I hear.

Frank That's right, Lottie and I don't care who knows it. I'm enjoying life — dominoes and darts and quiz nights ... karryoaker and trips out wi' t' lads — never been such times!

Mam snorts

Old tyme dancing on a Friday night, Lottie.
Mam (*with a tinge of envy and longing*) I'm surprised you can still do it ...
Frank (*doing a little shuffle*) Oh I've still got me rhythm, Lottie — and me thrust should need arise!

The women go "Oooh!!" and laugh

Mam Don't think you men ever lose it — more's the pity.

Frank stares at her fondly then notices that Dad is staring at him

Frank Evening, Jack. Howist?
Dad Been better, Frank. How yoursen?

Frank nods. Something old and uncomfortable passes between the men

Alice Well must be off, your singing sounded lovely from across the way — sound does carry this time of night doesn't it? (*With this mild reproof she heads for the door*) Toodle-oo for now then!
Dad (*happily*) Toodle-oo.

Alice exits

Mam (*matter-of-factly*) Alice Clegg. I went to school with her — she was man mad. Used to sit on wall by lads' toilet showing all she'd got.

Frank gets up and strolls closer to Dad who is gazing at Beulah. Heather moves DC *and inspects her reflection in a "mirror" — she pats and fluffs her hair*

Heather Must have a perm this week. Fancy coming, our Mary?
Mary A perm? Last perm I had was done with tongs and paper.
Mam You're a damn fool, our Mary, left with all them bairns and neither of the getters paying you a brass farthing.
Frank (*to Dad*) That's a grand photo Craig took.
Dad Ay.

Heather (*to Mary*) My John says you could take that Ray Gallat to court.

Mary Can't get blood out of a stone. Anyway he says he'd rather go to prison than work to give us money.

Frank Remember when we killed t'ord boar pig, Jack?

Dad nods, smiling in reverie

There was me an' thoo and Reg Bartlet, Piggy Fletcher wi' his cold chisel ... bah we had a tussle ...

Mam (*to Mary*) We told you he was a waster didn't we, Dad!

Dad (*his reverie broken*) Who's that?

Mam Our Mary's second disaster — that gormless Ray Gallat!

Dad Oh him.

Mam She would have him.

Mary sighs

All freckles and bulging jeans. (*Shuddering*) What drips we used to get trailing up to Beulah after her. Tom cats, *drips*!

Dad Eh? Bit late isn't it?

Mam Drips! After our Mary!

Dad I thought you said chips.

Mam Wasps round a jam jar they were. (*She looks at Mary suspiciously*) Lord knows why.

Mary Thanks, Mam.

Dad (*fretfully*) I wish I had my pipe.

Heather I'll have a look in the bedroom, Dad ...

She exits into the bedroom

Frank Poor ord Nelson, minute we opened sty door he knew we'd come to end his days.

Mary Nelson? We had a pig called Nelson?

Mam Frank christened him, daft devil ...

Frank He ran into my fork an' lost an eye — one morning when I was mucking out.

Dad (*slipping back into a reverie*) Talk about scream. Pigeons went clattering off down Dale, dogs started barking — cats ran into stockyard wi' their tails up.

Pause. The women regard their father sadly

Mam He's raking things over all the time. Wandering. He'll go back to Pontius Pilate if he keeps on.

Rene reaches out and strokes Dad's arm

Rene He's happy enough.
Mam He laughs in his sleep, jabbers on — you've never heard such stuff.
Heather (*off*) Eureka! I've found it, Dad!

Heather enters with Dad's old black pipe and goes to his side

Dad Oh well done, lass.

They all watch Dad clamp his pipe in his jaws and suck happily

Mam He'll be full of wind now, blowing me out of bed all night.
Frank "Bladder for a balloon, arse for a whistle", that's what Piggy used to say. "Nowt wasted but the squeal".
Mam He was a disgusting man.
Frank (*staring at her*) I can see you now, Lottie, walking across that yard with a bowl for neck blood to mek black puddings.
Mary I wish I'd stayed a vegan.
Mam Bit late for that isn't it?
Mary Veg*an*, Mam!

The others giggle

Meat disgusts me lately.
Mam Good job you didn't marry that Derek Watson then — Co-op butcher's man!

Laughter. When it subsides Mary glares at Mam

Mary You don't think I'm capable of anything do you?
Mam Capable of staring at ceilings ——
Rene Mam, that's enough.

Mam is chastened slightly. Slowly Dad stretches his thin white arms up towards the photo

Dad They bet us we couldn't carry Nelson from killing post to barn — remember, Frank? Never mind creel I said — me and Frank'll carry him across.

Frank *I* bet them we could, Jack, that was way on it ...

Dad looks puzzled and has to lower his arms weakly

Mam (*to Frank*) Just like you to clever off.
Frank Must've been twenty-five stone or more dead weight but we did it. Then we pulled him up over bath like a great steaming white shark — and Piggy undid his belly buttons for him.
Rene Urgh — Uncle Frank!

Frank laughs

I hated killing days. We used to shut ourselves in the back bedroom out of the way.
Heather And play records on that old gramophone ...
Frank Good days weren't they, Lottie love?
Mam (*snorting*) All I got was more work — baking for you men, great hungry-nosed beggars. (*But her voice has no edge*) Messing up the kitchen all day.
Dad I wish I could just close my eyes and find meself back at Beulah — just for ten minutes or so. I'd just like to stand on front step and smell wind coming up Dale — bit of beck sound in it or a bit of a sea-fret. Pine resin, sheep tar, heather. I'd give owt to hear them moorjocks calling on Scartops.
Heather Times I've offered to take you, Dad ...
Dad I know, I know ——
Mam He's in no fit state to go nowhere. He shouldn't be out of bed ——
Dad If I can walk to this couch I can walk to a car ... (*He throws the blankets aside, swings his feet to the floor and sits up. He gasps, and holds his chest*) Whoa up, Jack.

The women stare at him, sensing his pain. He grins through it at Frank, remembering

Remember Dabber Thompson, Frank?
Frank (*laughing*) Ay! Laugh? I had to lie down to laugh ——
Dad Dabber was first in Dale to get a tractor. "Little Grey Donkey" it was called — a Ferguson. None of us had seen one afore let alone driven one ... (*He grips his chest tighter and stares an appeal to Frank*) Frank.
Frank Dabber got plough yoked up and set off — (*steering an imaginary wheel*) went straight through two hedges and across another field into beck shouting, "Whoa! Whoa! Whoa up damn yer!"

The women laugh gently with the men; they've heard it all before but they don't mind. Mam remains deadpan, watching Dad work through his bout of pain

Mam Serves you right, laid conducting like that — now look at you.
Rene Are you all right, Dad?
Dad Bah, Rene lass, it hurts when I laugh.
Mam (*afraid*) You won't shape, you won't shape to get better that's your trouble — you've always been the same — great big man that you are you'd rather lie down than fight — you could get better if you'd fight!
Dad Lottie.

He passes his hands tenderly over his abdomen as Heather and Rene move to his sides

There's summat laid in here like a rough ord stone off a wall. Doesn't hurt much when it's still but when it decides to shift itself — bah, it canes me.
Mam (*agitated, not listening*) You've never fought or argued with a soul, Jack Ling — always been a soft touch, come day go day that's been you — yes, take it, oh have it — you'd given half our tackle away before the farm sale started!
Dad It's got me beat.

He stands with the help of Rene and Heather. Mam watches them. They head towards the bedroom door. Dad speaks without looking back

Night, contrary Mary, night, Frank.

Mary smiles. Frank looks sombrely after them

Frank Night, Jack.
Dad Don't be long, Lottie. (*Pause. He laughs*) I might have summat for you tonight.

Rene and Heather giggle

Dad, Rene and Heather exit into the bedroom

Mam (*snapping*) Just keep to your side! Don't be sprawled across my half when I come to bed.

Her face softens as they listen to the voices from the bedroom

Dad (*off*) Rene. My best lass. (*He grunts and sighs as he gets into bed*) And little Heather Ling. I'm glad you're staying a couple of days — we'll be able to watch *Emmerdale Farm* together tomorrow night.
Rene (*off*) Yes, Dad.
Heather (*off*) *Emmerdale Farm*, yippee!
Rene (*off*) Loves *Emmerdale*, don't you, Dad ...
Dad (*off*) Amos is my favourite, he teks a grand part.
Rene (*off*) Sshhh ...

Heather emerges from the bedroom

Frank glances at his watch. Mary stands wearily

Mary S'pose I ought to get back to the brood.
Frank Ay, mun gan meself, lass ...
Mam Who's looking after them bairns of yours all this time?
Mary Darren and Tracey ...
Mam They could all be burnt to death ...
Mary I've got to have some time away, Mam ...
Mam What for? I never had any time away from you lot ——
Mary Times have changed! Women are demanding lives of their own these days!
Mam Have you been going to them night classes again?

Mary groans. Heather grins

What rubbish have them posh teachers been filling your head with this time?
Mary Why do you hate to see me enjoying myself?
Mam Enjoying yourself is one thing, getting bairned by one dimwit after another — is another!

Rene enters from the bedroom and listens with her arms folded

Frank fidgets by the door, waiting for his moment. Mary is hurt

Mary Know what's been really scaring and depressing me so much lately, Mother?
Mam (*spooked by this formality*) Oh *Mother* is it? Having four kids by them two gormless beggars'd depress anybody ...
Mary I feel I'm growing more like you every day. Despite all my efforts I'm

growing into you — and I *hate it.*

She gets up and pulls Garry to his feet

Come on, Garry.

Mam gives a frightened crow of denial

Mam Rubbish! You're like him — (*glancing towards the bedroom door*) you get crazes, you joined the Sally Army when you were hardly big enough to bash a tambourine ——
Mary You never listen to me! There seems to be nothing I can do to make you see me as I am!

She kisses Heather and Rene hurriedly and tows Garry out past Frank, who is knocked slightly in her wake

Rene I'll give you a ring, Mary love ——
Mam (*singing and bashing an imaginary tambourine*) "Come and join us come and join us! For we're all as barmy as bats!"

She realizes the others are staring at her and stops. She folds her knitting and stands up, guilty but defiant. She notices Frank staring

I thought you'd gone.
Rene Mam, don't be rude ——
Frank It's all right, lasses, me and your mam go back a long way — don't we, Lottie?

Mam stares at him. He backs towards the door

Anyway, been grand. Mun gan though ——
Mam Mun gan? What language is that?
Frank (*struggling*) She used to laugh at things I said, lasses — I could always make her laugh couldn't I, Lottie love?
Mam Mun gan instead of "must go" has worn a bit thin over the years, Frank and I'm not your "love". Good-night.
Frank (*hit*) Ay ...
Rene You used to make us laugh, Uncle Frank, didn't he, Heather?

Heather blinks

Your turn at village concerts used to bring the house down.

Heather (*softly, wryly*) Or the Nissen hut down.
Mam I'm going for a bath then to bed.
Frank Want me to scrub your back, Lottie?

Mam gives him a withering look

Rene crosses to Frank and kisses his cheek

Rene Night, Uncle Frank.
Frank You remember my "turn" then, Rene lass? I'd forgotten it mesen ...
Rene Of course, it had us in fits didn't it, Heather?
Heather (*clueless*) Oh yes! Love to hear it again ——
Frank Gerraway?
Heather — sometime —— (*She crosses quickly and kisses him*) Night, Uncle Frank.

Uplifted, Frank exits

Heather turns and lets out a big sigh of relief

Turn? What bloody turn?
Rene Never mind, it went on hours — people were crawling down the aisles begging him to stop. (*She darkens*) Well actually, it scared me, as a child — one of those things that starts off funny then suddenly isn't any more. (*She stops and looks at the door leading to the bathroom*) Our Mam, honestly.
Heather I know, she gets worse. Sometimes I come here feeling quite happy you know?
Rene (*fondly*) Oh that's fatal, she senses that ...
Heather Mam, destroyer of egos, shatterer of self-esteem.
Rene The most tactless woman who ever lived.

They laugh softly together. Heather picks up her jacket from the back of a chair. Rene picks up a cup from the table and makes her way to the kitchen; she pauses to stare at Beulah. Heather watches her

Heather How's Ted?
Rene Fine. Thinking of taking early retirement. (*She sighs faintly*) Seems incredible that he once *ran* up that field to see me.
Heather (*teasing*) In his khaki shorts and plimmys.
Rene You remember?
Heather (*moving closer to Rene and staring at the photo as well*) We saw him.

Rene But. I was on my own, I looked up from the letter I was writing to him and saw him — from the bedroom window.
Heather (*pointing it out*) And Mary and Mam and Evie and me — were there — watching from the front room — (*with an accent*) from t' parlour lass eeh bah gum first boyfriend we'd seen ecky thump.
Rene I thought only I saw him.
Heather His first visit, poor Ted. (*She giggles*) Mam lines us up in the kitchen like servants — "This is my daughter Heather, this is Evie, this is Mary and *this* — (*fawningly*) is my *son* Craig."
Rene (*musing*) That was August and the following year we got married. It was so hot the wedding cake collapsed and the cars had to crawl over the moor road because of the dust. Ted and his best man were sweating buckets and the chapel windows were wide open.
Heather He was sweating when he finished shaking hands with us lot——
Rene I dragged him off to the front room ...
Heather Soon as the door closed Mam said: "I'n't he *little*".
Rene (*laughing*) You rotten lot!
Heather Oh we liked him — 'specially Craig.

Pause. They stand arm in arm gazing up at the photo

Rene Dear old Beulah. Such happy times.
Heather Before bloody reality caught up with us, eh?

She kisses Rene and slips away towards the door. Rene remains, cup in hand, gazing at Beulah. Heather pauses

You were lucky finding a man like Ted weren't you, Reen? You've had a good marriage haven't you?

Rene glances at her with a smile. Heather smiles back

Night then.
Rene Good-night.

Heather exits and closes the door behind her

Rene's smile turns sad and dies. She stares at Beulah for a moment longer then heads towards the kitchen door. She is chased by darkness as the Lights swoop down into a Black-out

Scene 2

The same. Mid-afternoon, one month later

Heather is looking at Easter cards on the table idly. Mary is sitting by her. Mam is at the window, peering over the lace

Mam Seen my Rhodies, Heather?

Heather puts the cards down and stares

My Rhode Islands, pecking about on lawn.
Heather What?
Mam I could only afford three but I might get some more next week ...

Heather frowns, puzzled

Hens! Hens! They sell 'em in Coopers.
Heather Hens. In the ironmongers?
Mam They're the latest thing ...

Heather looks at Mary: is this senility at last?

Mary (*placidly*) They're metal, painted hens you stick in the ground.

Heather goes to the window and stares out

Mam Well?
Heather I'm overwhelmed, Mam.
Mam (*snorting*) We need a bit of life about the place. I might get a dozen next week!

She glares at her daughters defiantly and moves C, *agitated, her eyes going to Beulah*

Gallivanting off like that. How much longer are they going to be?
Mary You could have gone — Evie offered.
Mam No point trailing back up there, it's gone all that — finished.
Heather Funny isn't it, I've offered to take him, my John's offered — oh no no — but as soon as Evie comes.
Mam They'll be bringing him back stone dead.
Mary Don't say that ——

Heather Mam's right, he shouldn't be bouncing round those Forestry roads in his condition.
Mary I thought he was looking better ...
Mam He's failing every day. I've written our Craig to get hisself up here if he wants to see him.

Mary and Heather are stilled by this, and stare out front

He was riddled when they opened him up and here he is — joy-riding.
Heather I'm surprised at our Reen letting him go.
Mam I'll never understand how a man as healthy and clean-living as him came to be riddled with maligerant tubers, never.
Heather Tu*m*ours, Mam.
Mam Oh ay you reckoned to be a nurse — you tell me?
Heather Don't start, Mam ...

Mam snorts and goes into the kitchen. We hear her bang pots and pans about unnecessarily

Heather When was Craig here last?
Mary Christmas.

Mam pokes her head around the kitchen door

Mam He can't just drop things, he's an important man.

She withdraws

Mary and Heather look at each other

Heather The brood all right?
Mary Seething. How're yours?
Heather Fine, Nick loves college — hey I think I've persuaded my John to buy me a little Peugeot at last!
Mary (*flatly*) How nice.
Heather Well he hates me driving the Sierra so I said to him ——
Mary (*cutting in*) Does he like being called "My John"? — sounds like a cross between a Labrador and a toilet.

Heather goes tense and bites her lip. Pause. Mam bangs on in the kitchen

(*Calling*) What are you doing, Mam?

Mam (*off*) Getting his Complan ready ...

There is the sound of people entering the bungalow

Mary Sounds like they're back ——

Mam zooms out of the kitchen and flops into her chair. She starts to knit unconcernedly, this time a blue balaclava.

Mam Make way for the coffin.
Mary *Mam* ——

Rene is first through the door, edging sideways

Rene (*helping Dad in*) Here we are, Dad, back home safe and sound.

Evie and Dad enter. Dad is between Rene and Evie — he looks ashen, windblown and triumphant

Dad I'm back, Lottie.

Mam knits on regardless

Rene He's enjoyed it so much, haven't you, Dad?

Rene and Evie help him to the couch

Dad Wouldn't have missed it for owt.
Mam You look about fit for maggots.

Rene sits beside Dad on the couch as he catches his breath. Evie kisses Heather

Evie Heather, you do look well.
Heather So do you — lovely dress.

Dad looks across at Mam, weak but elated

Dad Eeh, Lottie love, we went up by Lockton and looked clean out over Dale to Beulah.
Mam (*her anger giving way to curiosity*) Looks like it's knocked your end in an' all ——

Dad Sun came out and beck was glinting like glass through them sycamores in t' bottom. Then great shadows of clouds went galloping across our fields and over the house.
Mam Frank says some bloke from Leeds has it for holidays ——
Dad Looked just the same didn't it, lasses?

Rene nods

Evie Apart from the h*oo*rendous plastic picture windows — hon*estly* (*she stares at Beulah print*) putting those things in a lovely old house like that.
Mam Butcher from Leeds has it Frank reckons ...
Evie Make it look as if its eyes have been picked out ——
Mam He's got one of them soona baths where cow-house used to be ...

Heather and Mary giggle

Forestry's planted fields up wi' conifers and stone walls are broken down, Frank reckons ——
Dad (*vehemently*) Frank Frank Frank!

They stare at him, shocked. Pause. Mam continues to knit

Air was same anyroad. Smell of peat and bracken and sheep — you can't beat that tang of moor air.

He tosses his words like stones at Mam, desperate for a response, a hit

We stood by Evie's car in the wind. Wheels were dusted wi' pollen. Gorze flowers and catkins out on banksides — I've never felt so happy for a long time.
Mam Doctor'll go hairless if he finds out.
Dad A steam train went up before we left. Tourists hanging out of every window — not like when it was a proper service — you could set your watch by them trains up and down' Dale.
Mam You've never had a watch — (*to the others*) watches don't go on your dad.
Dad Trains were a grand help if you were working out in fields. Me and Frank'd have our snap when twelve train went up.
Mam Lucky doctor didn't call this aft ——
Dad Bugger the doctor!

They all stare at him, amazed by the swear word. Mam heads for the kitchen in triumph

Mam I expect he's ready for summat to eat ...
Dad Drink, woman! I'm dry as snuff.

Mam exits into the kitchen

Mary stands up

Mary I'll have to go and stoke the brood ...
Evie (*kissing her*) Bye, Mary love, see you before I go I hope.

Mary smiles, kisses Dad and heads for the door

Mary Bye, all ...
Dad Bye, contrary Mary.
Mary (*pausing*) Started to call me that haven't you, Dad, after years and years.
Dad You were contrary in your cot — wasn't she, Lottie?
Mam (*off*) And before. Worst pregnancy I had and worst delivery — like getting corn beef out of a tin.

The others laugh

Mary makes a face and exits

Heather regards Evie

Heather Back to the ord hearth then, our Evie eeh bah gum ecky thump. How was it?
Evie Afraid I disgraced myself in the car, didn't I, Reen?
Rene (*smiling*) Big baby.
Evie When Dad pointed out the track we used to take to school — I just broke up.
Rene Those were happy days. Setting off together bright and early across the woods and fields.
Heather Not all of them. Mam once sent me off with my frock on inside out ...

Her sisters laugh, remembering

I went through hell that day.
Mam (*off*) I did no such thing!
Heather She did, I realized just as we were setting off: "My frock's on inside out," I said in horror.

Dad Five miles there and back in all weathers. You were hardy bairns ...
Heather "Off you go!" Mam said, "It's bad luck to change it back!"
Mam (*off*) I never did.

Mam enters with a bowl, stirring the contents

You were always romancing, Heather.
Dad Not that stuff again, it's like calf meal, Lottie!

Heather intercepts Mam and takes the bowl and spoon from her

Heather Let me, Mam. (*She sits beside Dad*) Come on now, it's full of essential vitamins.
Dad It's nowt but wind and watter, lass.

Heather spoon-feeds him. Mam watches them

Mam I'm going to wash my hair.

She exits

Dad Her hair was harsh and black as a Gallowa's tail when we first moved into Beulah. I mean, when she first came to live there when the old folks were alive—she used to wash it in rain-watter from that barrel outside back door.

Heather nudges Dad's lips with the laden spoon

Heather Open up, Dad.

He takes it and masticates slowly

That's the ticket.

Evie stares across the room at Beulah

Evie Like a time warp up there, wasn't it, Reen? That world we knew, all there but distorted, subtly changed — village school turned into a *bijou* holiday cottage, Methodist chapel into an "outdoor pursuits centre", whatever that is.
Rene Remember the chapel anniversary every year?
Evie Tell me about it! It was the only time we got a new frock each.

Rene I used to dread going out to the altar to say my "piece".

Evie (*giggling*) I quite enjoyed it — all the boys and men in their white shirts, hair slicked back — and the women and girls in flowery frocks. Oh and the chapel freshly lime-washed and hung with roses, do you remember?

Rene (*remembering*) Wild roses trailing from the beams and huge old ones pinned to the sheets along the altar rails. You never see those old Damasks and Bourbons now — the smell made you dizzy when you got out to the front.

Heather In your little cotton socks ...

Rene Little did I know I'd be standing there years later in my wedding dress — legs trembling just the same.

Evie (*softly*) I thought the legs trembling bit came later, our Reen ——

Rene shushes her as they laugh. Evie stands, clasps her hands coyly, turns her knees inward and recites in a little shy girl's voice

Evie "We thank you for the Springtime, Lord
For birds and trees and flowers
For running brooks and humming bees —
For sunny happy hours."

She flounces into the chair again, mock embarrassed and delighted

Rene That *was* your piece! What a memory.

Evie laughs. Heather spoons Complan into Dad. He stares at Evie suddenly

Dad Tek your coat off, lass.

Evie Oh, of course!

Dad (*laughing*) I'll not tek me coat off I'm not stopping! Al Read, I used to like Al Read on wireless: "I'll not take me coat off ——"

Evie (*putting her coat on the back of a chair*) I'm not stopping — right, Dad.

Heather (*eyeing it*) Lovely bit of schmutter, sis.

Evie Oh Colin keeps me nice — (*with an edge*) he likes me looking just so.

Pause

We entertain quite a lot.

Rene (*gently*) How are things?

Evie shrugs but looks suddenly hurt, vulnerable

Evie I've got the kiddiewinks and he doesn't knock me about or keep me short — far from it.

Rene and Heather look sympathetically at her

Mam returns with a damp towel arranged like a turban on her head. She stands C, *rubbing her hair dry*

Mam Water's that hard down here — makes my hair go like sticks.

Dad sits with his mouth clamped shut

Heather Dad, you must eat.
Mam (*afraid*) Open up for nursey, the six months wonder. Couldn't stand emptying the bed pans and breaking her nails, could she!

Heather glares at Mam

Rene Mam, that's not fair ——
Mam Used to come home crying about kids in iron lungs — you've got to be tougher than that I told her — you've got to be hard to be a good nurse!
Heather Oh I've got harder, Mam, but you can still hurt me, can't you? I'm the one who's looked after you the most you know. I'm the one you always send for — and never a bloody word of thanks ——
Mam (*hurt*) Thanks? Who brought you up, madam — who slaved after you for years on end?
Dad Is it Good Friday soon, Lottie?

This prosaic questions stills them all

Rene Tomorrow, Dad.
Dad I thought so, have to be sorting out some tatie sets.

They all regard him sadly

Allus put some sets in on Good Friday — weather permitting.
Mam Where are you going to put them — in the window-box?

The sisters roll their eyes at each other. Rene sighs. Heather tries Dad again with a spoonful of gunge

Heather Dad. It's good for you ——

Dad (*pushing the spoon away*) Think I don't know what's good for me, lass ...? (*He stares across at Beulah*) I've had God's first fruits all my life, in their own good time as their season swang round — brambles in white enamel buckets from Beulah's hedges, bramble pies and jellies and jam thick enough to choke a bullock, great hairy yeller goosegogs and Victoria plums and home baking twice a week, new taties coming out of that black moor soil like bunches of pale white grapes ... I've lived at Harvest Home all my sodding life, lass. (*He calms a little, staring at them painfully*) Don't tell me what's good for me, I'm not a bairn ...

Heather At least you can keep this down, Dad ——

Dad (*flaring again*) It's baby pooh!

Rene You must eat.

Dad Eat? I could eat any man under the table in my prime. Yorkshire puddings and gravy — I'd eat six big uns on a Sunday dinner-time. Sadcake and treacle, bramble wine and rasp pie and full-cream milk still warm from cow, curd tarts and brawn and beef dripping, pig chap, honey from the comb ... (*he is in pain, holding his abdomen and starting to retch*) all the fat of the land and fruits of the earth ——

Heather (*panicky*) Mam!

Dad — salted butter, home-cured hams ... fat bacon and bread baked in side oven for break'ast ——

He stops as Mam wipes his lips with the towel from her head. She stands over him as he recovers. Heather looks chastened and stares into the bowl on her lap

Mam You shouldn't have taken him up there! Nobody takes any notice of me — I told him not to go — stupid man.

She looks a fright, with her damp hair all over the place. She looks harshly at Heather

Mam! Mam she says — fine nurse she'd have made.

Rene Are you all right, Dad?

Dad (*nodding*) Where's our Craig?

Rene He's coming, Dad, don't worry.

Dad We used to get on you know. He'd come looking for me and Frank soon as he got up — trotting across fields — he'd find us, stonewalling or summat. His face'd light up when he saw us ...

Rene Yes, Dad.

Mam walks towards the window, wiping her hair again with the towel. Dad stares after her

Dad She wanted to stop after Mary but I said we'd go on till we got a lad ...
Mam And what did you do with him when you got him?
Dad Eh. What d'you mean, woman?
Mam (*staring over the window lace*) He was made for better things than plugging muck and walloping cows — he wasn't cut out for it.
Dad I wanted to learn him. I wanted to.
Mam You let Frank tease the life out of him — he was slight like me. (*She mimics Frank*) "He's ower heavy for light work and ower light for heavy ... ", times he came in upset, crying wi' cold or summat ...
Dad To a house of damn women — ay! You made him that soft, you ruined him.

Mam turns and gives him a bitter glance. She moves towards the exit

Mam I'm going to shift my hens on to some fresh grass.
Evie What hens?

Evie and Heather move to the window and pull down the lace

Heather Her funny metal hens — they don't lay a lot but she likes them.
Evie (*with an Harrovian inflection*) Not those things stuck in the grass. Mother ho*nestly* ——
Heather (*getting her own back*) They're surrogate hens I suppose — speckled surrogates!

Mam turns, nettled

Mam Leave my hens alone. Anyway it's (*deep Yorkshire*) grass lass — not gr*auss*.
Evie (*nettled*) I have lived in Harrow nearly eighteen years, Mother dear ——
Mam (*painfully posh*) Ew we noew that, Miranda — we're very lah-dih-dah noew aren't we? Lots of brauss and coins for the gauss noew, haven't we?

Rene struggles between mirth and anxiety

Evie Honestly. You can't bear to think I've got away from you and bettered myself can you!

Mam blows a full raspberry

I come back here with the best of intentions — feeling like a real person and before a day's out I feel like a ... (*staring about for inspiration*) a ——

Heather Snotty-nosed naughty little brat again?
Evie Exactly! And you wonder why I don't come back very often, Mother, why wild horses wouldn't drag Colin up here!
Mam (*snorting*) Too busy seeing to his fancy women I expect ——
Rene Mam that's enough ——
Mam He's got nowt to be stuck up about — big head, typical Southerner.
Evie Mother, you're impossible.
Mam We've never liked him have we, Dad ...?
Dad (*cluelessly*) No no.
Mam I'll never forget our Evie coming back from the Army three months gone. Silly bonny lass — throwing her life away on *him.*

Evie stands, flabbergasted

It nearly killed me.
Heather Heavens' sake! That was decades ago ...
Mam I was at top o' stairs polishing the banister rail when she told me. She stood at bottom snuffling and I said, "What's up wi' you, miss?" — as if I didn't know. "I'm pregnant, Mam," she said and I nearly fell backwards all the way down.

The sisters collapse into laughter, C, *shaking their heads and holding each other. Dad stares, bemused*

Blummin' Southerners! Moving up here in droves now after fouling their own nests — after scorning the North for years! I hear 'em in the post office with their grauss and pauss — and a*uss* I shouldn't wonder!
Rene (*still in fits*) Oh, Mam!
Mam (*heading for the exit*) Oh pauss me the auss paper will you, Miranda — ew hain't there henny? Then pauss me a handful of grauss there's a good lauss ... (*She yanks the inner door open in a tizzy of anger, enjoyment and, possibly, shame*) I speak as I bloody find! Always have and always will ...

Alice and Craig enter

Alice Ah there you are, Lottie — this young man's looking for you.

Mam stares, smiles and blossoms almost coquettishly in the doorway

Mam It's my son.
Alice Really ——?
Mam (*in a strangely posh voice herself*) Oh yes it's my Craig — I've got four

daughters and Craig who works in London. A photo journalist.

The women look at each other as Mam embraces Craig like the Queen Mum

Craig, how are you?

Craig puts down his case and lets himself be embraced by this damp, wild-haired woman. He grins over her shoulders at his sisters

Craig Hallo, big sisters.

He looks across the room to Dad

Dad.

Black-out

Scene 3

Sunday afternoon, a week later

Dad is lying on the couch, blanketed, staring up at Beulah. Craig sits on a chair at the end of the couch, staring at the sunny curtains. Rene moves about in the kitchen, off, preparing something and humming

Long pause

Craig Mam's still keeping a bit of livestock I see.

Pause. Dad turns to look at Craig

Hens, out there.

Dad nods. Silence

Dad I'm going home, lad.
Craig (*puzzled*) But I thought this ... Oh. Yes, Dad.
Dad Gine yam. (*He chuckles sadly*) You've forgotten dialect I reckon?
Craig Not a lot of call for it in Wapping, Dad.
Dad Gine yam. It's gine yam ... they made us talk "proper" in school but as soon as we go' outside them gates it was gine yam, bugger scheeal, swearing and cossin' all' way — *yam*.

Craig smiles and nods

Couldn't put wo'ds like them in your paper eh, lad? Nobody'd understand!

Craig No.

Dad You' Mam cuts your articles out. She's got them all filed away — I understand they're very good.

Rene appears in the kitchen doorway smiling and stirring Complan in a bowl

I'm hungry, lass.

Rene On its way, Dad.

She goes out

Dad I don't read papers any more. World gets out of all kenning. I don't know what went wrong, lad — we seemed set fair after war when we all got back to work. What a state of affairs. (*He shakes his head wearily*) Families breaking up, men and women hating each other—bairns being abused. All this S-E-X and life made cheap as muck wi' killing. I don't understand it, lad.

Craig No, neither do I ...

Rene enters with the bowl and puts a towel across Dad's chest. She sits on the couch beside him with spoon at the ready

Rene Oh dear this is serious talk.

Dad This is my best bairn. Best loving daughter a man ever had ...

Rene (*laughing*) Dad really ...

Dad How things turn round eh, lass? Doesn't seem five minutes sen I was feeding you with a spoon at that kitchen table at Beulah ... (*He stares at the photo*) I wish it had been mine to leave you bairns.

Rene Oh never mind that ...

Dad That's my worst regret. Forestry gave us chance of buying it once but we didn't have cash. We never had cash at right time ...

Rene (*spooning*) Let this stop your nonsense.

Dad accepts the Complan and chews it sadly. Rene glances up at Beulah

Rene Know what I used to love? Waking up on Sunday mornings at Beulah with the sun on the bedroom curtains and Dad singing as he cooked breakfast. Always cooked breakfast on Sunday didn't you, Dad ...?

Dad More.

Rene (*feeding him*) I always felt so safe and happy. The sun and the smell of bacon frying and you singing to yourself. (*She softly sings Richard Tauber's "Girls Were Made to Love and Kiss"*)

Craig watches her, smiling, but he is slightly embarrassed

Dad More.

Rene (*spooning more into his mouth*) Isn't it nice to see Craig, Dad? You should be proud of him ...

Dad Oh he's done well for himself. (*Hit, he seems oblivious to Craig's presence*) I must have offended him somehow though. (*Like the old comedian*) Hey have I offended you? No have I? Have I offended you? (*Pause*) I used to like Al Read on the wireless ...

Mam enters talking, leading in Heather, Evie and Frank

Mam There has to be wars to keep the population down! We'd be standing on each others' heads now if it wasn't for wars!

Heather and Evie stand and giggle. Mam smiles at Craig

If I was Prime Minister there'd be some changes!

Heather and Evie laugh and hoot derision

You can mock — if I could have my time over there'd be some changes round here!

Evie You wouldn't have had us for a start?

Heather We know you'd have been happier with a few calves and hens ...

Frank That right, Lottie?

Mam Wouldn't come into it because I'd be born a man ——

Heather } (*together*) { Boo!
Evie } { You traitor!

Mam goes to the window and peers over the lace, showing off to Craig

Mam A real muck or nettles man I'd be — I'd travel the globe all on my own. America, Alaska and across the Canadian Rockies — I wouldn't be tied down or beholden to anybody. I'd make a career for myself. I'd be my own man and speak my mind like ... (*she casts around for inspiration*) like ...

Evie Robert Maxwell?
Frank Brian Clough?
Heather Jack Charlton?
Mam (*waving two fingers lightly back at them*) Like Harvey Smith!

They all laugh. Rene gives Dad more Complan. Mam crosses the room and looks at him

Dad More.
Mam He's a bottomless pit.

Craig notices Frank beaming at him and stands up

Craig Hallo, Uncle Frank ...
Frank (*shaking hands*) Nay you can drop "Uncle" now, lad, I reckon you're old enough! (*He stands back and regards Craig dubiously*) I don't know, lad, you don't put any meat on do yer? Seen more meat on a butcher's biro!
Mam Don't talk so daft.
Frank I said we owt to call him "Reck" when he was born didn't I — reckling! He was that poor ——(*he laughs*)

Craig looks mortified

— I didn't think he'd live!
Dad More.
Mam He's like Oliver Twist.
Evie Did the doctor call yesterday?
Mam (*nodding*) "There's life in the old dog yet, Mrs Ling," that's all he said. Crew-cut hair and leather jacket — more like a mugger than a doctor.
Dad More.
Evie He can't be so bad, all the food he's putting away ...
Rene Been eating like a horse for three days now, haven't you, Dad?
Mam (*heading for the door*) Feeding for the grave.

The women stare at her in horror

Evie Mother you are the limit ...
Frank Where you off now, Lottie?
Mam Going to shift my hens, don't like 'em where they are.

She exits

The women regard each other. Frank moves to the window to peer out over the lace. Dad repeats, over and over, in same obdurate tone: "More"

Evie Ever thought our Mam missed her vocation — as a Macmillan Nurse?

They titter

Heather Such patience. Compassion.
Rene She hates illness, remember when we were little — off school with mumps, all of us?
Heather She used to come into the bedroom with that scarf round her mouth ...
Evie Throw us a few scraps and back out again. How did we all survive?
Heather (*drolly*) *Did* we all survive?
Dad More, more.

Rene feeds her father

Frank (*murmuring*) Lottie Gregson.
Heather Come again, Uncle Frank — Gregson?
Frank (*moving across to them*) As she was like. You bairns think you know your mother but — (*he shakes his head, staring at Dad*) bah she was a bonny flighty little thing. The day she came up to Beulah to meet the old folks she had a cream dress on and a straw hat wi' them artificial violets on the brim, eh, Jack?
Dad More.
Frank We were real thrang sowing corn so I met her at Levisham Station wi' pony and trap. As we drove down lane to Beulah hawthorn blossom was blowing across us like snow. An' smelling like sick ...

He chuckles

She was capt wi' it — "Like confetti," she shouted in my ear: "Just like confetti!"
Heather (*lugubriously*) Eeh bah gum ecky thump — obvious what was in her mind then eh?
Rene Hear that, Dad? She meant to have you, eh ...

Dad doesn't seem to hear. Frank stares at his profile

Frank He meant to have her. Wasn't long afore they were wed and you were on your way, Rene — then he went off to join up like.

Mam enters and moves to Dad

Mam You all right, Jack?
Dad What night is it?
Mam It's Sunday afternoon. (*She turns to the others*) He's worse today. Where's our Mary?
Dad We allus have a singsong Sunday nights.
Mam Him and his hymns. Proper old Sankey Methodists the Lings were, eh Frank? They wouldn't let you do a hand's turn on Sundays once fires were lit and beasts fed.
Frank (*laughing*) I used to say to yer mam, "Don't set your backside on fire Lottie, nobody'll put you out today!"

Mam giggles and her daughters stare at her

Heather I think we ought to get the doctor out.

They all gaze at Dad who seems very, very still all of a sudden but for his right hand as he conducts some tune within his head. He stares at Beulah

The Lights go down to denote a passage of time

The Lights come up to reveal of room of vigil. The curtains are drawn and the only light comes from a lamp on the sideboard and through the bedroom door, which is ajar. Craig and Heather sit in chairs. Heather is manicuring her nails. Evie sits on the couch, leafing through a magazine. Rene sits by Dad's couch. There is a mood of sad expectancy — they are all intent on the halting murmurings of their father

Dad Frank. What sorta stean is that? I want flat steans. I telled tha ... (*Pause*) There's allus another day — nowt gotton in a rush but unwanted bairns and bad hay, didn't tha hear Faither say that? (*With effort, as if he was lifting something*) That's more like it, son. Now thoo's shaping ... there's allus a stean to fit son think on.

Craig stiffens slightly and stares at Dad

Some steans rock and some sits. (*He chuckles*) Some "claps doon" Faither used to say — just like an ord hen when' cockbod goes by. He's shaping better now, Frank, he's getting hang of it ...
Evie What does he think he's doing?
Craig (*tautly*) Stone walling. Mending the walls — don't suppose there's a drink in the house?

Heather Was there ever?
Craig (*looking around*) How did they bring us up? They had nothing.
Heather Everybody had nothing so it didn't matter that much.
Dad (*suddenly harsh*) I'm telling tha, Frank ... (*he mumbles something indistinct but hard and dark: a dire warning maybe?*) I'm not (*rhyming it with "sinned"*) blind — I'm telling tha. There'll be a reckoning day.

Rene shushes him

Rene There, Dad, don't get upset. Shush.
Dad There's summat bothering me, Rene lass ...
Rene Mam'll soon be back ...
Dad I keep thinking. *Wondering*. There's summat on my mind ...
Rene What is it, Dad?
Dad The grandfather clock's for you and Ted. Sorry I've nowt much else for you ...
Rene Is that all you're worrying about? I don't care about that — you've been the best father anyone could have wished for.
Dad No not that. I wish I knew summat but I can't imagine.

Mam enters with Mary. She looks childishly sombre. She stares at them

Mam Well?
Heather He's just the same, Mam, talking — wandering a bit.

Mary moves closer to Frank by the window. Mam glares at her

Mam She had him dead soon as she saw me on step. "It's Dad," she said with eyes like saucers. "He's gone, hasn't he?" Seen too many blummin' TV films ...

They all look at Rene as Dad whispers to her

Rene There's something bothering him, Mam ... can't seem to leave it be?
Mam (*shrugging*) How should I know?
Rene (*with a tired edge*) I just thought you *might*.

Mam snorts and stares through the window as if she'd like to jump through it and run away

Mam I'll be glad when he's got his time over.

Pause. They stare at her, shocked

(*Shouting*) Summat about religion I expect, well it's no good asking me!

Heather Stop shouting!

Mam (*after a pause*) Well. Proper Oh-Be-Joyful he's always been underneath — all his side were that way — and I hated it.

She looks at Frank

Dad (*urgently, sombrely*) Rene lass.

Rene leans close to him. The others listen

What do *you* think, Rene?

Rene How can I say, Dad, when I don't know what's on your mind?

Dad murmurs something which they all strain to hear but fail to catch. There's a pause, then Rene giggles, splutters slightly hysterically and looks at the rest of them, hand over mouth, caught between tears and mirth

Mam (*agitated*) What's he say, our Rene?

Frank Ay, what's he say?

Rene He's that concerned —— (*She giggles again and stops herself*) He says: "What is going to happen on *Emmerdale Farm* next week ...?"

They all laugh, united for a moment and relieving their anxiety, then they dry up. Frank looks at Mam. Pause. Everyone moves slowly to form a tableau, like a family portrait. The Lights begin to dim

Dad Whoa wharve Maisie bring 'em round dammit. Bring 'em round. Thoo great soft Gallowa'. (*He mumbles and laughs like a confused but happy child for a while*) Gerraway by Bess — get! Get back, dog. Fetch 'em in gently. (*He whistles*) Gerraway *by*! Bah. (*He gives an enormously long deep languorous sigh*) Knew he would tak' it away from me. Said pain would leave me at finish. God I love tha and thank tha for a grand life, grand days — had the best of it I reckon — can't complain at all. *Eh* it's been bloody marvellous.

He dries up. Mary slumps, her elbows on her knees and her face hidden in her hands

Mary He never once asked to see me. I've been here most days but he never once asked me to do anything for him.

Dad (*brightly*) Is it Sunday night?
Mam Yes, Jack ...

Dad rumbles something indistinct. Pause. Rene stares at them

Rene Shall we sing his favourite hymn?

They stare blankly at her

Shall we?
Mary I can't ——
Evie (*shaking her head*) I haven't sung for years — what is it anyway?

Rene looks at Heather a moment. Then Heather starts to sing, "How Great Thou Art". She is shaky at first then confident and strong, full of a kind of innocent, girlish desire to please. It becomes a plain and beautiful rendering

Heather
O Lord my God
When I in awesome wonder
Consider all the works Thy hand hath made —
I see the stars, I hear the mighty thunder —
Thy power throughout the universe displayed.
Then sings my soul my Saviour God to Thee:
How great Thou art
How great Thou art.

Rene starts to sing too. Mary stands with Evie's arm still about her and they join in the soaring second verse. Frank sings. Craig watches them dumbly

Heather
Rene
Mary
Evie
Frank
(*together*)
When through the woods and forest glades
I wander —
And hear the birds sing sweetly in the trees
When I look down from lofty mountain grandeur
And hear the brook, and feel the gentle breeze —

Frank nudges Craig into song

All
Then sings my soul my Saviour God to Thee:
How great Thou art
How great Thou art.

They are grouped around Dad's still figure in tableau as the singing reaches its height

Then sings my soul my Saviour God to Thee:
How great Thou art
How great Thou art!

They sing as the Lights dim

Black-out. Silence

ACT II

Scene 1

The same. Afternoon, three days later

Heather is by the window looking out expectantly. She is dressed in chic funeral clothes. At her side, but on another planet, Garry stands with his Walkman and does a kind of robotic hand-jive, eyes glazed. There are sherry and scotch bottles, glasses, sandwiches, sausage rolls etc., on the table

Heather I think the cars are here.

Mary enters from the kitchen. Her funeral clothes are a strange mixture

Mary Kettle's almost boiling.
Heather Yes it's them. (*She turns back into the room*) Always a lot of people with dandruff at funerals aren't there? Black shoulders speckled with it everywhere. (*She watches Mary*)

Mary strolls up to Garry and pulls at one of his earphones

Mary Sid*down.*

Garry sits

Heather You didn't mind not going to the graveside?
Mary Not really.
Heather (*chewing a mint*) Have you ever heard such a naff sermon? He seemed to be talking about gardening all the time.
Mary (*pouring herself a scotch*) I can't remember what he said. It all seemed ... surreal to me.
Heather Something about us all having to be cast on to the great compost heap at the bottom of God's wonderful garden — (*she giggles*) in order to melt down and be born again ... Pour me one will you?

Mary pours another scotch

Mary I kept thinking: why do I need their approval? I'm a grown woman, why do I keep desperately trying to please them?

Heather I suppose we all do, except Craig ... even our Reen seems to need that.
Mary (*handing Heather the scotch*) Reen's always had it — always been their favourite.

They turn as they hear the other mourners entering; Mam in black raffia bonnet on Craig's arm, followed by Frank, and Rene and Evie in their weeds

Heather Are you all right, Mam?
Craig She's cold, it was bitter at that graveside ...
Mam That minister was a disgrace. He knew nothing about your dad.

Craig takes Mam's coat and she sits in her usual chair. The others take their coats off and pile them on his arm. Mary sits in the carver chair

Frank He was new to the game if you ask me.
Rene Good turn out anyway.

Craig puts all the coats on the couch

Frank A lot of t' ord Dales' folks came to see him off ——
Mam I don't know how some of 'em dared show their faces. That Joe Garthwaite still has a set of harness he borrowed off your dad.
Craig Sherry anyone?
Evie I'll have a large scotch, I'm frozen.
Mam He didn't know your dad from a hole in the ground.

The sisters regard each other. Pause

Craig Would you like a sherry, Mother?
Mam Might as well, I'm paying for it.

Craig sorts out some drinks at the table. The women find chairs

Rene There were some wonderful wreaths.
Frank Sorry I was a bit late into chapel, Lottie ——
Mam Late? You nearly missed it.
Frank I popped into *George* for one and sorta lost track o' time ...
Mam I could smell your breath three rows in front.

Craig distributes the sherry, watched hopefully by Frank

Heather I take it my beloved's still in the *George*?
Frank Ay. (*Longingly*) Him and Ted and Ray Gallat — drinking like ducks after a thunderstorm.

He catches Craig's eye and nods towards the drinks

Craig Scotch, Frank?
Frank Ay, why not.

Craig pours Frank a drink. Frank is immensely cheered by this and beams at the women

And how's my Heather honey? I christened you Heather you know ...
Heather (*giving him a look*) I hate it, especially coming before Ling.
Frank Ling's a good ord Yorkshire name, lass ——
Evie Thank God you didn't christen one of us Vera.

Craig hands Frank his drink

Frank (*laughing*) By heck I never thought of that!
Mary They used to call me Ting-a-Ling at school.
Evie Evelyn Ling. Who'd have put those two together?
Heather Uncle Frank apparently. He christened the doomed boar Nelson, he christened ——
Frank Your mam gave me that honour ...
Craig Craig doesn't really go either ...
Mam (*snorting*) So you're all unhappy with your names! What else did we do wrong?

The women grin and chuckle. Craig downs his scotch and pours another

(*Grimly*) I think I can safely say Jack would have been disgusted with his funeral.

The women look at each other. Heather rolls her eyes

I don't know who that organist thought he was.
Frank Elton John, I reckon.

The women giggle

Mam He had sun-glasses on. Galloped through "Abide With Me" as if he had a train to catch. Half of us were trying to keep up and t' other half trying to slow him down — I felt quite giddy at one point!

Frank Well. (*He is ponderously sentimental*) He's out of all harm now, Lottie. He'll be able to lie there and see clean over to Scartops and listen to sheep and curlews calling.

Mam Don't talk such tripe, he won't be seeing or hearing owt anymore.

Frank (*dashed*) Nay well — depends on how you look at it I suppose.

He downs his drink and moves to Craig's side, glass in hand

Craig lad.

Craig fills his glass

Craig Frank.

They both find themselves lost for words. Pause. Frank dredges up a thought at last

Frank I look through posh papers every Sunday for your pieces an' photos. They get sick o' me in t' paper shop ...

Craig smiles politely

By heck I did you a favour all them years ago, eh lad?

Craig (*puzzled*) Sorry?

Frank That box Brownie I bought you for your eighth birthday — surely you've not forgotten?

Craig Oh no, no.

Frank (*beaming*) I had to send away for it, lasses. Ten and six was money in them days — but what an investment, eh?

The women grin. Frank downs his scotch, blows his cheeks a bit and holds his glass out for more

Got him off on his brilliant career, right lad.

Craig fills his glass

Always popping up with his little Brownie at the ready, wasn't he, lasses?

The women giggle at this image

Proper pest at times ——

Heather (*nudging Evie*) Know the feeling, sister?

Evie giggles

Mam "A blessed release, Mrs Ling." That's what that barmy minister said to me — what's he know about it?

Rene It's over now, Mam ...

Frank Ay we can't do it again ...

Mam chills him with a look, then looks at Mary

Mam Get up and let your Uncle Frank sit down, before he falls down.

Mary I'm not a kid, Mam ——

Frank I'd rather stand as it happens ——

Mam (*snapping*) Sit down, Frank, you're getting me all on edge hovering about with that glass!

Mary vacates the old carver chair. Frank sits in it and claps a big hand on the arm

Frank This ord chair. Me faither spent hours in it when he was failing — sat staring into fire like an ord collie dog.

Mam I want you to have it, Frank, there's nowt else.

Frank That's kind of you, Lottie ...

Heather Actually Dad said I could have the carver ...

Mam First I've heard.

Frank To tell you truth, Lottie there's summat I'd rather have — if it's all same to you.

Mam Grandfather clock goes to Craig ——

Rene stares at her but says nothing

— owt else you can fight for when I'm gone.

Evie (*grinning*) Bags the ducks then!

The women and Craig laugh

Frank Yon picture of Beulah — I'd be capt ti deeath wi' that.

They all look at the picture. No-one speaks

I dwell on them times up there. When all you fine lasses were bairns and I was living in. Can't remember what happened last week but them days is clear as. (*He shakes his head and stares at the picture*) When Faither died and Jack took over tenancy we had barely a shilling to scrat our backsides wi' so Jack said we'd plant a field o' taties for a good cash crop. About ten acres there was and me and Jack stood looking at it wi' them two ord mares yoked to a one furrow plough. (*He laughs*) I coulda rooared. Then all of a clatter and a shout Joe Todd comes through gate wi' his ploughing team, and mid-morning Dick Fletcher towed up wi' his, and some bugger I can't think of his name. "Come to plough you in," Joe shouted and started opening up a flap ...

Mam Gordon Waind from Moor-End Farm.

Frank That was the man. Talked all of a splutter: "Wuwheer do yu-you want me to start, Jack?"

Evie giggles and holds out her glass, which Craig refills. Frank holds his glass out and Craig refills that as well

Anyroad, by about two o'clock that big field was shining brown from wall to wall. Folks used to help each other in them days — we all had nowt much but we shared it around. (*Drinking*) Ta, Craig lad.

Craig What a lot we've lost, haven't we. That easy generosity, tacit rural solidarity. It'll never come again, will it?

Heather (*flip*) Why did you leave it then? You couldn't wait to get out of the Dale.

Craig I wouldn't say that ——

Heather Dad offered you all that ...

Craig (*hit*) I'm not a farmer — besides, farms of Beulah's acreage were hardly viable even then.

Heather He was offering you a way of life not a business plan.

Craig I had my own plans ...

Mam Farming's jiggered, he was right to leave.

Frank You're right, Lottie, there's nobbut dairy men making a decent crust these days.

Craig I didn't want it. (*He knocks back more scotch*) I've never fitted into the mould of horny-handed son of the soil ——

Heather All right! But don't come back cracking on about rural life ——

Rene (*big sister*) Now you two, remember what we're here for.

Craig and Heather visibly sit on their feelings

Mam Craig's made a success. (*She stares at her son*) The only one of you far as I can see.
Craig Mam. (*He shrugs apologetically at his sisters*)
Mam I can't get over Jack. (*Musing*) I think he must have had a knock sometime and kept it to himself. Lings were bad healers — flesh like ripe fruit the old lady once said to me — if Jack got a bruise it'd be on him for days.

She shakes her head; everyone watches her

I thought he'd want to be cremated being full of tubers like that. I know this much — I'm not going in on top ... (*She stares at them darkly*) Think on you lot — I want burning.
Rene Yes, Mam.
Frank Do you want gas or electric?

Laughter; Mam glares at him

Mam Behave, Frank Ling or I'll turf you out. (*She takes her hat off at last and gets up stiffly, tiredly*) Think I'll have a lie down.

She stares at Garry, who is still sitting, zomboid, by the bedroom door

They don't say much, young uns, do they?

Mary pulls at one of Garry's earphones

Mary (*snarling*) What do you say to your granma?
Garry (*blankly but pleasantly*) Get a life, Gran?

Mary glares at him

Rene shepherds Mam out to the bedroom

Craig pours himself another scotch and Mary offers the sausage rolls around. Frank is the only one who takes one. He bites into it with gusto

Frank Grand lass, Rene. Topper.
Mary (*wearily*) Yes we know.
Frank Grand woman your mother. Don't think our Jack really knew what he'd landed hissen there.

Mary Caught her fishing did he?
Heather Wished he'd thrown her back a few times.
Frank I could never see 'em as a match — couldn't see 'em in harness.
Evie (*cheekily*) Harness, Uncle Frank? Was that the latest thing?
Heather Kin*ky*.

Frank chuckles, enjoying their gentle teasing

Frank She danced once. She danced to music at village concert ... just her and that ord gramophone on stage — there was a bit of talk about it — and Jack was fuming. He was bad to work with for days after.
Heather Our mam danced?
Evie On *stage*? Shock horror.
Frank This was before any of you were thought of — and I tell you summat for nowt: she lit that ord village hut up.
Evie Not as much as your "turn", Uncle Frank!

Heather switches on the lamp and turns it towards him like a spotlight

Heather (*in a heavy Yorkshire dialect*) An' now from Beulah, home of the famous Family Ling, we present Frank Ling with his incredibly popular monologue — (*she scratches her head*) what the heck was it called?

There is giggling and applause

Frank "Song of the Moffrodite Cockbod". And if you think I'm doing if after all this time ——
Evie Oh please, Uncle Frank! We could do with a laugh.
Mary I've never heard this, why haven't I? It's a family legend I've missed.

Rene enters

Rene What's all the noise?
Evie Uncle Frank's going to do his turn — isn't it exci*ting*!

Mary and Heather yawn exaggeratedly. Craig refills Frank's glass. Rene looks uneasy

Craig Not going to disappoint us, Frank?

Frank downs the scotch and moves C, *with the light from the lamp on him. The others applaud and even Garry takes his Walkman off to pay attention for a few moments*

Frank I deean't know. I'm out of pocket ageean. I allus ends up outa pocket somehow — y' see I thowt I'd go into poultry trade an' bowt thirty-five young Rhodies off this ord Moor-Ender i' Malton Market. Why. I knew he was t' sort that'd skin a Mowdie and then skin skin but why, I fancied messen as a bit of a hegg tycoon. Me name's Willie frae Stape by the way.

They all giggle

(*Aside to the family*) I shoulda said that at start. Onnyroad, I puts bods in a run and feeds 'em reglar but after a bit I realize I've been done — t'ord bugger's gi'n me thirty cockbods an' five pullets i'stead o' t' other road round. Why, what di yer deah?

The women giggle. Evie pretends to be asleep

Them poor little hens nivver gat a minute's peace. The "Frantic Five" I called 'em because they were soon bald wit' cockbods pulling feathers out their scourps and going bare back wi' 'em getting on and off — I mean, them cockbods was on and off like Christmas tree lights — in fact it warn't lang afore three on 'em tonned their toes up i' protest in a corner o' t' run. I was crazed. Now there warn't enough broncos ti keep cowboys going and — (*he looks around shiftily*) they started stanning about wi' queer looks i' their een if you get me? Then yar day it musta come tiv 'em because they were at it — they were on and off yan another regardless — the scrawny bad buggers had tonned Moffrodite!

The women hoot now. Craig shakes his head ruefully

Why, what di yer deah? I necked 'em all but yan and buried 'em in a mass grave at back at house. So I'd come down ti yar Moffrodite cockbod an' two pullets — then yan o' them took a run at fence and damaged itsen so bad I had to pull it's neck an' to'ther gat cropset like Snowcem' so I necked it an' all. See what I mean about being outa pocket? Onnyroad I gat sick o' seeing the "Last of the Moffrodites" as I called him parseling about run so I decided to neck him an' 'e done wit' poultry trade altigither. Bugger had gotten wary though and I couldn't round him up so I waited till dark and went with me torch to catch him on peak so to speak. I snuck up ti t' henhouse and let pophole down and knew I had him — me fingers was fair itching to hev hodden his neck — but then ... I heard this noise ... there was this noise coming out o' t' darkness inside ... I had a change of heart. As I stood gawping and gobstrucken under stars I felt mercy driving murder out of my heart and I knew me fortune was made. I'm not kidding you — that Moffrodite cockbod was *singing*.

The Lights are tinged with blue and start to fade as Frank starts to croak like a cockerel, Wagner's "Ride of the Valkyries" with immense vibrato, feeling, pathos, bathos, angst, you name it. The effect is hilarious but oddly chilling

(*Seriously, deadpan*) Poak poak poak ... *etc*.

The women are still, silent. Craig and Rene look blanched, lost in reverie. Garry lifts his earphones from his ears and regards them as if all his worst suspicions about adults are confirmed

Frank builds his poultry song to a crescendo. The stage is bathed in blue light

Black-out

Scene 2

The same. Later that night

It is pitch black outside. Craig stands before Rene with his jacket off and tie loose. His tongue has been loosened by drink; he talks as if he didn't care, but beneath it all there's pain

Craig So. That's the state of play. I'm giving her grounds and we're separated — she's got Sylvie and Lottie and I've got a room in Camden that's costing me an arm and a leg.

Rene I am sorry, Craig.

He drinks; she watches him

Craig Oh I'll survive. You just ...(*He shakes his head*) You begin to wonder what's wrong with you. Aren't you capable of making another person happy?

Rene Dad would have been upset, he was fond of Claire. "Like one of my own lasses," he used to say. (*Pause*) You didn't tell him?

Craig shakes his head, downs his scotch and goes to the table for a refill

What did he say to you?

Craig shrugs

Did you say anything to him?

Craig Not a lot. (*He walks* C *with the scotch*) *Like* to have said: "Sorry for not being the strapping farmer's son you'd have liked — sorry for being a bloody disappointment ——" (*He slugs back the scotch and gasps*)

Rene You chose a different life that was all ——

Craig (*suddenly harsh, his accent returning*) Oh ay, I "got on" — I "made summat of mesen". (*He laughs shortly, and stares at Rene*) Claire's going with this bloke — colleague on the rag actually — *I* introduced her to the boasting sod.

Rene Oh.

Craig (*ruefully*) It's strange. I'm almost as hurt by her lack of taste as I am that she left me — he is such a *prat.*

Rene (*at a loss*) Well.

Craig I thought she was happy. I'm away a lot but I thought we were doing all right — two kids, detached house on a decent estate, two cars, two holidays abroad per annum ... (*Pause*) She said there was nothing there any more. (*He thinks about it, then shrugs wearily, baffled*) "Nothing there."

Pause. Rene stares across at Beulah for a moment. Craig watches her

What's the secret, big sis? How do you make a marriage work?

Rene Why ask me?

Craig Come on, you're an example to us all — we all admire you and Ted.

Rene turns away and starts to clear the table

Rene We've had our ups and downs like anyone else.

Craig (*gently mocking*) You've had rows with Ted? Nay nay — you'll be telling me Pope's turned Methodist next!

Rene (*turning*) None of you know what it was like for us. Ted had to finish his National Service before we could get married — then I went back to Beulah while he saved and saved and stayed in lousy digs until we had the deposit for a house! It hasn't been easy.

Craig sees that she is hurt, goes to her and takes her arms

Craig (*brotherly*) On'y kidding, our Reen.

She smiles wanly

Rene It's been a long day.

Craig Ay. (*He moves away, puts his glass on the table and picks up his jacket. He regards her fondly*) Still at the centre, big sis, still trying to hold us all together.

Rene I don't know about that.

Craig Who else remembers every birthday and loves family reunions, and Christmas — and writes and phones regularly.

Rene Well I was the first, I was waiting for you all when Mam brought you home. You were the *bonniest* baby ...

Craig I peaked too soon.

They smile. Pause

I hope you and Ted are all right. I'd hate it if you and he ——

Rene We won't. (*She regards him*) Still a bit wary of Uncle Frank aren't you? I know how you feel. Always been a bit wary of him myself. (*She stares at him*) How could two brothers be so different, Dad so kind and gentle and Frank — such an old rake!

Craig shrugs uneasily

Rene He's mellowed a bit thank goodness, but he was an awful tease. He could really get on your bones.

Craig Sticks and stones. Not true is it. (*He stares at Beulah*) "Reckling." When he said that I was back in the yard that morning. They were laughing, I came round the corner and they were laughing as they hauled Nelson up above that wooden bath. Blood dribbling from his snout and neck. There's a photograph of me somewhere on that pig's back.

Rene I know.

Craig Piggy took his evil little knife out and I stared at the ground ... I heard it all plunge into the bath — lumps and coils — a heavy splashing. Then I ran round the corner again and was sick.

Rene I'm not surprised.

Craig Dad came round the corner and (*proffering a hand to the air*) said, "Away back, lad," but I couldn't go back. Uncle Frank was shouting, "What's up wi' Reckling Jack? Fetch him out!" I ran away, and stayed away — watching from the trees until they'd all gone.

Rene You were at a difficult age.

Craig "Reckling" — poorest of the litter. It got to school somehow and became my nickname.

Rene embraces him

Rene We never thought of you like that.

Craig (*smiling*) Ted saved my life in a way. Quick, clever man from the town — he taught me judo holds and we made a balsa wood glider.

Rene I remember.

Craig I once saw you run down the front field into his arms — skirts and hair flying.

Rene (*laughing*) It was the most wonderful coincidence! I'd been writing this letter to him at my dressing-table, wanting him — missing him so badly and suddenly there he was.

Craig I read the letter.

Rene stares, hit

You ran past me on the landing and I mooched into your room and saw your letter and then you running down the field. The side mirrors were turned inwards and I could see my thin doomed reflections stretching away into infinity. (*Pause*) Sorry, big sis.

Rene shakes her head

Craig "My dearest love, I cannot tell you how much I am longing for the day when we will be together as man and wife — how I yearn for the night in which I shall give myself to you utterly, for ever, without shame or doubt or conditions." (*He stares at her sadly*)

Rene You were just a boy ...

Craig I wished I hadn't read it, it shattered me, Rene — the world seemed to turn inside out. (*He laughs softly*) I realized Ted had a bit more on his mind than balsa wood gliders. It scorched my mind that letter. The commitment of it, the surrendering of yourself — it was too powerful.

Rene (*regarding him with clarity, as if for the first time*) You're a deep un, little brother.

Craig Deeply boring ...

He moves slowly towards the door, stops and stares at it. Rene follows

Will Mam be all right?

Rene (*nodding*) That bed seems enormous.

Craig Frank once said. We were up the top field mending walls. I was fetching stones — I put one down with a finger under it and burst into tears. "Thoo's gotten a lad that shoulda been a lass, Jack," he said — and for years after I thought Mam's womb had got so used to shaping girls it only stuck me a willie on at the last minute.

He hugs Rene and they laugh softly together

(*Soberly*) I'm not terribly at ease with my male colleagues and my female ones treat me like a brother. (*He grins ruefully*) Some things never change.

Rene Ted. Just won't talk about us at all — "If it's going all right," he says, "don't mend it."

Craig And it is all right?

Pause. There is a touch of frustration in Rene's voice

Rene All right.

Craig There's some stability left in the world then!

He gives her a departing squeeze and goes to the door. He looks back with a fond smile, relieved

Good-night, Rene.

Rene (*fondly*) Good-night.

Craig exits

Rene remains staring at Beulah for some time as the Lights fade. Black-out

Scene 3

Morning, three months later

The Lights come up as summer sunshine, flooding the room. There are summer flowers in a vase on the table. Heather, in jeans and shirt, is dusting, humming to herself. After a moment Mary enters carrying a shopping bag and an envelope

Mary Heather.

Heather Mary.

Mary Cleaning up.

Heather So observant — you should have been a writer or something.

Mary (*pleasantly, dumping bag on table*) Sarky bitch. (*Looking at the letter*) Looks like Craig's writing.

Heather Well done, brother, three months since Dad died and he's managed to put pen to paper. Surprised he didn't set Mam up with a fax machine ...

Mary (*staring around*) Is she out again?
Heather Mam or the cat's mam?

Mary scowls. Heather nods to the bedroom door

In her boudoir getting tarted up.
Mary What's got into her?
Heather Ecstasy? Demonic possession? You tell me.
Mary I've heard of late flings but this is ridiculous. I came round three times last week and she wasn't in.

Heather exits and returns with a floral aerosol spray

Heather She's got a Green Rover and a Red Rover and a barrelful of bus tokens. Monday she went to Whitby — (*spraying*) hence the lingering niff of kippers. Wednesday it was York Railway Museum, Thursday the Elderbugs outing to Castleton Market.
Mary (*flapping the spray away*) She's joined the Elderberries?
Heather What! She's a leading light now, or is it a "Boss Berry"? They're going on a mystery tour today.
Mary (*oddly irritated*) Where on earth to?

Heather regards her sadly, slowly and revolves a finger beside her head, waiting

Oh I see.
Heather Haven't we been sleeping again?
Mary (*sighing*) Since you ask. Ray came round last night, pissed as a rat and crying — he wants to try again — but I can't.
Heather Don't even think about it!
Mary (*sighing*) Love, Heather. It's just a lottery isn't it.
Heather Mm — I'm beginning to think Patience Strong hasn't quite grasped all of it in her poems myself.
Mary I did feel sorry for Ray.
Heather Mary he's a ... (*She stops herself*) He's a builder's labourer, sweetie. He wears jeans that don't cover his buttocks — *think* about it?

Mam puffs in from the bedroom in her best cream frock. She wears a cardigan and an old straw hat with faded artificial violets on the brim. She carries a handbag. Her face is flaking with make-up

Mam (*routinely*) You look awful, our Mary.

Mary Thanks, Mam.
Mam Peaky, crow's feet, bags under your eyes — are you opening your bowels regular?

Mary just stares at her, destroyed

Think I'll need my coat, Heather?
Heather It's roasting out, Mam.
Mam Cardy'll do then. I think I've got everything. (*She her opens handbag and checks her purse*) Mm. I hope we aren't going round by Blue Bank — it terrifies me.
Mary You're gadding about a bit.

Mam goes to the window and peers over the lace

Mam Her from number seven's out waiting already. Hope we get an inside seat. Sun gets fit to roast you through them windows. (*She looks back at Mary*) Your dad never took me anywhere. (*Looking at Beulah*) Never wanted to be anywhere but that place ...

Heather hands Mam the letter

Heather From our Craig.
Mam (*stuffing it in her bag*) I'll read it on coach if I get chance. I haven't forgiven him yet — leaving them lovely bairns — him and her want their backsides kicking.
Mary What's the point of living in misery with someone you no longer love?
Mam (*snorting*) Love, you're always on about love. You've spent so much time picking your lives over you've forgotten about living 'em!
Heather Thank you, Dear Marje ——

Heather and Mary start giggling

Mam You can giggle! We're here for a short stay then it's curtains and a merry wind to our arses!
Mary What a philosophy — the Sage of Beulah has spoken.

Mam moves in front of the picture and stares at it

Mam You all go on about that place as if it was heaven on earth. It was a prison to me.

Her tone stills them; they stare at the picture

There were times I could have torn all my clothes off and run across them fields screaming —— (*she stops with an effort*) But I did what I had to do. I kept my vows.

Mary I thought you were happy enough.

Mam Did you really take any mind? Mam, that was me, Mam putting grub on table, Mam washing mucky clothes, crabby old Mam bent over that peggy tub — what's she want wi' dreams? What's she want wi' a life of her own?

Mary (*shocked*) Mam.

Mam Ay! Mam mam mam mam mam mam, (*she gives a shout of immense frustration and defiance*) MAM!

Pause

You think you know me — but there was a man I could have had — (*she snaps her fingers*) just like that — I could have had another life ...

Heather (*shocked*) What? Who ...?

Mam (*shaking her head*) There was someone. First time we met I knew ... he took my fingers in his for a couple of seconds and I felt — singing alive — singing in my head ... blood rushing like a singing swollen beck between my ears ... and a kind of certainty and peace. (*She gets hold of herself*) That was the only time we ever touched apart from a daft kiss at Christmas, things like that.

Heather Oh, Mam.

Mam (*angry with herself*) I shouldn't have told you ...

Heather You were so lucky, you should have gone to him — run away together!

Mam That's easy said.

Heather God! *I* would, I'd have. Crawled over plains of broken glass for a love like that ...

She falters. Mary stares at Mam, struggling to absorb the news

Mary After all you've said to me. You had a lover.

Mam Lover my backside! We never even spoke of it, we got on with our lives — but we *knew*.

Heather And Dad?

Mam shakes her head

Mary I'd have gone with him. Every day at some point I reach a pitch when I want to scream: to hell with the brood — *I want my own life back.* I'd give anything to be loved properly, for myself — for what I am. I feel my life bleeding away every day and nothing happens ...

She stops as she hears someone knocking and entering the bungalow. Mam goes to Mary's side

Mam A son's a son till he finds a wife but a daughter's a daughter all her life ... (*She smiles with rueful tenderness at Mary*) Bairn that's most like you causes you most pain, our Mary.

She pulls Mary's head down against her chest for a moment then steps back as:

Uncle Frank enters, smiling and spruce in his summer linen jacket, with coloured hankie sprouting rakishly from his breast pocket

Frank You ready, Lottie? Bus's waiting.
Mam (*smiling radiantly*) I'm ready, Frank.
Frank (*offering an arm*) Let's be off then.

Mam ignores his arm and heads for the door

Mam Lock door when you leave, our Heather, and put key in coal-house.
Heather (*weakly*) Have a nice time.
Frank Nowt so sure, Heather lass. (*He winks at Mam*) Going all the way this time aren't we, Lottie love?
Mam Daft devil — what are you on about?
Frank Why — (*laughing*) no good getting off at Seamer if you're going to Scarborough is it!
Mam (*pulling him towards the door*) Come on, you know what coach driver's like ...
Frank Looks like a bloody Moffrodite to me ....

He does the poultry version of "Ride of the Valkyries" as Mam tows him out. We hear them leave the bungalow

Heather and Mary look at each other, stunned, then go to the window and peer out L

Mary Can you see them?
Heather There they go, last ones running to the bus.
Mary Running? Oh yes ...

Heather She's holding his arm now, be Jaisus.

They watch incredulously, confused

They've made it.

Mary walks to a chair and flops into it. They stare at each other, realizing

Mary Honestly. Our mam.

Black-out

Scene 4

The same. Two months later, a bright sunny morning. Bird-song

Heather is taking the ducks down carefully. On the table c *are boxes, old 78 records and the wind-up gramophone with its lid up. The Beulah picture rests across the arms of a chair* DR. *Mary is winding the gramophone up. Heather brings two ducks to the table*

Heather Wait till our Evie gets these through the post — (*she quacks comically*) her dinner guests will *love* them — such *taste*, Evie darling! Oh *yah*!

Mary smiles. Heather gets the remaining duck

Mary (*looking around*) What junk. No wonder we never got in *Homes and Gardens*.

Heather "flies" the duck to land on the table, quacking again

Not much Laura Ashley, not very Sanderson — not even bloody G-plan.
Heather (*calling off through the door*) You OK, Reen?

Rene emerges carrying a shoe-box with no lid and tips the contents — ten or so small, cheap diaries — gently on to the table. They each pick one up

Mary What's this?
Rene Dad's diaries. They were in the wardrobe ...

Pause. They leaf through pages

How small his writing was.

Heather (*reading*) "Periwinkle on service" — Periwinkle?
Rene (*absently*) Cow.
Heather (*mock hurt*) No need to be like that ... (*She giggles and reads*) "All off school with measles — Mary very bad poor lass."
Mary (*groaning*) Why did I get everything worst ...? (*She picks up another diary*) Nineteen forty-two — good grief.
Rene "Lime-washed all buildings for young stock. Sunny and fair."
Heather Riveting stuff, isn't it. "Stone walling with Frank all day. Fine and mild for time of year." (*She turns the page*) Hang on! Sixteenth September nineteen fifty-nine — in big capitals: "Our dear Rene had a son born this day. Both well thank God. Fine but cold wind."

Rene takes the diary from Heather and reads, smiling

Rene That was our Jack, his first grandchild ...

Heather tosses a diary back into the box. Mary stares into hers

Heather Shan't make a fortune out of publishing these.
Rene I'd like them, unless ...?
Heather Have 'em, Reen.

Rene looks at Mary, who is still engrossed in her diary

Rene D'you want any of them, Mary?

Mary stares. She looks stunned

The diaries?

Mary shakes her head. Something makes Rene snatch the diary lightly from her grasp

What've you got there?
Mary Don't, Reen ——
Rene Nineteen forty-two. The year Dad came back from the war — you know I could never imagine him a soldier.

She reads on. Mary looks desperately across her at Heather, who looks puzzled

He must have been so happy to see Beulah again.

Alice bustles in

Alice Sorry to barge in but I have to check the gas and water ——

She exits into the kitchen

(*off*) — you will leave it clean and cleared of their old stuff won't you? We've no storage facilities and you know what the dustmen are like ...

She enters

Well that's all right then.

She regards them and the boxes, etc.

Rene Yes, don't worry.
Alice I'm not worried, dear, but the new couple move in next week and I don't want any complaints. (*She peers at the Beulah picture*) They weren't a lot of bother I'll say that for them. In fact he was a nice old chap.

Pause

She could be a bit short but never mind.
Mary (*watching Rene read*) She spoke her mind, our mam.
Heather Yeh, she didn't suffer twerps gladly.

They both stare at Rene who looks upset suddenly

Alice Mm. I suppose that's the way to go if you've got to go, isn't it.
Heather (*drily*) On the back seat of a bus half-way to Cleethorpes?
Alice Better than dragging on for ages with no control over anything I always say.
Heather (*coldly*) Do you really?

Alice senses the atmosphere at last and turns towards the door

Alice Right, drop the keys in when you're finished. (*She pauses beside Beulah*) Frank never got his picture, did he? I suppose he was a comfort to your mam in her last months but all the gadding about. (*She shakes her head*)
Heather (*flatly*) She died in his arms anyway.

Alice (*as she leaves*) Toodle-oo then.

Alice exits

Heather (*as the outer door closes*) Toodle-oo, you impervious bat.

Mary moves to Rene's side in concern. Heather picks up a record

Heather Did we really listen to this stuff? (*She puts it on the turntable*) I suppose it was either that or Uncle Frank's turn ... (*She moves to stare at Beulah*) You want this, our Mary?
Mary I haven't got a wall big enough — you have it.

Heather considers it a moment then shakes her head. She drifts back to the table

Heather Looks like you get the picture, Reen.
Rene Oh I get the picture.

Anguished, she stares past them at Beulah

The full bloody picture — at last.
Heather (*tutting*) You want your mouth washing out with soap, my lass ——
Rene (*cutting in, harshly*) Listen to this. (*She reads from the diary*) "I can't say anything. I can't and they won't and I think we all long for things to be as they were. Butter wouldn't melt — but I see it all now, years back — my brother and my wife. Do they think I'm deaf and blind as well as stupid? I work with my back to Beulah and dread going in. Something inside me is turning to stone!"

She stops, in pain and stares at her sisters

You *knew*.

Heather and Mary exchange guilty looks

Heather (*gently but irritated*) What planet are you on, our Reen? You know Mam and Uncle Frank were at Beulah for two years on their own ...
Rene So?
Heather (*turning away, fiddling with the gramophone*) So — do you think they just played whist every sodding night.
Rene (*hit*) I don't believe it ...

Alice is suddenly at the window, tapping, her voice a bleat against the glass

Alice You won't forget these, will you? She should have asked permission but I didn't say anything — I mean if everybody started sticking animals in the lawns — soon be like a farmyard out here!
Heather What is she on about?
Mary Those bloody hens — Mam's Moffrodite cockbods.
Rene Go away, you stupid woman!

Mary and Heather stare at her as Rene brandishes her fist

Go away! Go forth and multiply!
Alice Well, it's true what they say — breeding will out ——

Rene rushes to the window and is restrained by her sisters

Rene Our Mam had you weighed up, Alice Clegg!
Mary Yeh! (*In Mam's voice*) "Man mad she was — sat on lad's toilet wall showing all she'd got!"
Alice (*furiously*) She'd no reason to think so much of herself! When Jack got called up we knew it'd soon be Frank's turn up at Beulah — oh ay! (*She points at Rene*) It's a clever bairn that knows its father!

Rene gasps

Alice leaves

Mary (*whispering*) What does she mean. Heather?

Heather stares dumbly, holding on to the gramophone like a raft as the record starts to crackle on. Mary looks at Rene, who is transfixed C *with the diary held to her bosom. She beats the diary with her fist gently*

Is she saying — our dad wasn't — our dad? *Reen* ——

Rene shakes her head slightly, staring towards the window

Rene Just me. (*Pause*) I'm ... (*She stops and sighs*) *Frank's*. Had to be me of course — goody-two-shoes, the favourite. Look for perfection in this life you're asking for all you get ... (*She starts to break up*) All I ever wanted was for everybody to be happy, for everything to be — nice. (*She stares*) *Dad*. Uncle Frank. I've got *nothing left* ...

At last the Richard Tauber song "Girls Were Made To Love and Kiss" pours its scratchy liquid notes into the room. The music swirls about the three women as they absorb the information. They are close but isolated and very still — each is pained in her own way. The Lights fade as the song fills the room

Black-out

CURTAIN

FURNITURE AND PROPERTY LIST

ACT I

Scene 1

On stage: Lace curtains
3 plaster ducks
Grandfather clock
Couch/*chaise-longue*. *On it:* cushions, blankets
4 farmhouse chairs (one of carver type)
Wind-up gramophone
78 records
Table. *On it:* cup, magazines
Large photograph of "Beulah" farmhouse
Knitting needles, blue wool, half-finished balaclava, etc. (**Mam**)
Judge Dredd comic (**Garry**)

Off stage: Old black pipe (**Heather**)

Personal: **Garry**: chewing gum, Walkman
Frank: watch

Scene 2

Strike: Red wool and balaclava

Set: Easter cards (**Heather**)
Blue wool and balaclava (**Mam**)

Off stage: Bowl with Complan, spoon (**Mam**)
Damp towel (**Mam**)

Scene 3

Strike: Easter cards
Bowl and spoon

Offstage: Bowl with Complan and spoon, towel (**Rene**)

Personal: **Heather**: manicure set

ACT II

Scene 1

Set: Sherry and scotch, glasses, sandwiches, sausage rolls, etc.

Personal: **Garry**: Walkman
Heather: mints

Scene 2

On stage: As Scene 1

Scene 3

Strike: Sherry, scotch, glasses, sausage rolls, etc.

Set: Summer flowers in vase
Duster for **Heather**

Off stage: Shopping bag, envelope containing letter (**Mary**)
Floral aerosol spray (**Heather**)
Handbag (**Mam**)

Scene 4

Strike: Flowers/vase

Set: Boxes, etc.

Re-set: Gramophone and 78 records on table

Off stage: Shoe-box containing 10 small, cheap diaries (**Rene**)

LIGHTING PLOT

Interior. The same throughout
Practical fittings required: standard lamp

ACT I, Scene 1

To open:	Full stage lighting; evening effect, no light from windows	
Cue 1	**Rene** heads towards the kitchen door *Quick fade to black-out*	(Page 14)

ACT I, Scene 2

To open:	Full stage lighting; mid-afternoon effect	
Cue 2	**Craig**: "Dad." *Black-out*	(Page 26)

ACT I, Scene 3

To open:	Full stage lighting; afternoon effect	
Cue 3	**Dad** stares at Beulah, conducting with one arm *Lights fade to denote passage of time. When ready, bring up evening effect; light from standard lamp and through door only*	(Page 31)
Cue 4	**All** form a tableau *Lighting begins to dim*	(Page 33)
Cue 5	**All** sing final lines of "How Great Thou Art" *Fade; black-out at conclusion of hymn*	(Page 35)

ACT II, Scene 1

To open:	Full stage lighting; afternoon effect	
Cue 6	**Evie**: "Not as much as your 'turn', Uncle Frank." *Standard lamp effect as* **Heather** *shines it on* **Frank**	(Page 43)

Cue 7 **Frank**:" — that Moffrodite cockbod was *singing*." (Page 45)
Bring up tinge of blue. Start to fade normal lighting as **Frank** *sings; by the time the song reaches its climax, the stage should be bathed in blue light*

Cue 8 **Frank** finishes singing (Page 45)
Black-out

ACT II, Scene 2

To open: Full stage lighting; night effect (pitch black outside windows)

Cue 9 **Rene** stares at Beulah (Page 49)
Fade to black-out

ACT II, Scene 3

To open: Full stage lighting; bright summer effect through windows

Cue 10 **Mary**: "Honestly. Our mam." (Page 54)
Black-out

ACT II, Scene 4

To open: Full stage lighting; bright, sunny morning effect

Cue 11 As "Girls Were Made To Love and Kiss" fills the room (Page 59)
Slowly fade to black-out

EFFECTS PLOT

A licence issued by Samuel French Ltd to perform this play does not include permission to use the Incidental music specified in this copy. Where the place of performance is already licensed by the PERFORMING RIGHT SOCIETY a return of the music used must be made to them. If the place of performance is not so licensed then application should be made to the Performing Right Society, 29 Berners Street, London W1.

A separate and additional licence from PHONOGRAPHIC PERFORMANCES LTD, Ganton House, Ganton Street, London W1 is needed whenever commercial recordings are used.

ACT I

No cues

ACT II

Cue 1 The Lights come up on SCENE 4 (Page 54)
Birdsong (throughout scene)

Cue 2 **Heather** holds on to the gramophone like a raft (Page 58)
The crackle of a 78 record begins

Cue 3 **Rene**: "I've got *nothing left ...*" (Page 59)
Richard Tauber's "Girls Were Made To Love and Kiss" plays from the gramophone; increase volume as the lights fade

PRINTED IN GREAT BRITAIN BY
THE LONGDUNN PRESS LTD., BRISTOL.